ISATA KANNEH-MASON

Piano Inspiration

Book 2 | Grades 7-8+

Edited by Richard Jones
Fingering reviewed by Ruth Gerald
Music origination by Julia Bovee
Cover photography by Paul Cochrane
Cover design by Daniel Knight, danieldoesdesign.net

First published in 2023 by ABRSM (Publishing) Ltd, a wholly owned subsidiary of ABRSM

© 2023 by The Associated Board of the Royal Schools of Music
ISBN 978 1 78601 491 7
AB 4115

Printed in England by Caligraving Ltd, Thetford, Norfolk, on materials from sustainable sources
P15974

A note from Isata

I'm so happy to share with you *Piano Inspiration: Books 1 and 2*: my very own repertoire collections for intermediate and advanced pianists. They are filled with pieces that I love for many different reasons – you'll find some of my favourite classical piano pieces, music influenced by jazz and folk, tunes from stage and screen, and some wonderful works that aren't widely known. I've selected music by some truly inspirational female composers and composers of colour, and I'm particularly thrilled to present two new works by Natalie Klouda and Errollyn Wallen, along with my own *Waltz* – all composed specially for these books.

As a child, the notion that Black, female composers existed would have been a complete and joyful surprise to me – it wasn't something I was aware of at all! In adulthood, I've discovered some glorious music by inspirational women from past and present times. It was important to me to include works by Eleanor Alberga, Florence Price and Errollyn Wallen in *Piano Inspiration* so that other players may discover these wonderful composers earlier in their musical journey than I did. Composing is a passion of mine and I'm privileged to include my own piece alongside those of women I admire so much.

When putting together these collections, I wanted to feature music that played an important role in my childhood as a budding pianist. My teacher was always setting me a Scarlatti or Mozart sonata to learn, and this was an important part of my musical development. Some of my earliest experiences of performing were in piano exams and competitions. I performed Schumann's *Knecht Ruprecht* (Book 1) in my first ever piano competition, and I remember finding this piece – and the whole experience – both exciting and turbulent! Debussy's *The Little Shepherd* (Book 2) holds a note of nostalgia for me, and I find the harmony in bars 24 and 25 particularly beautiful. I played it in my Grade 7 exam and have recently relearnt and recorded it for my album *Childhood Tales* (Decca, 2023).

It has been a delight to compile these collections of piano pieces that are so special to me, and I hope that they bring you a great deal of joy, inspiration and musical discovery.

Contents

Mazurka in B flat

Op. 7, No. 1

Frédéric Chopin
(1810–49)

© 2023 by The Associated Board of the Royal Schools of Music

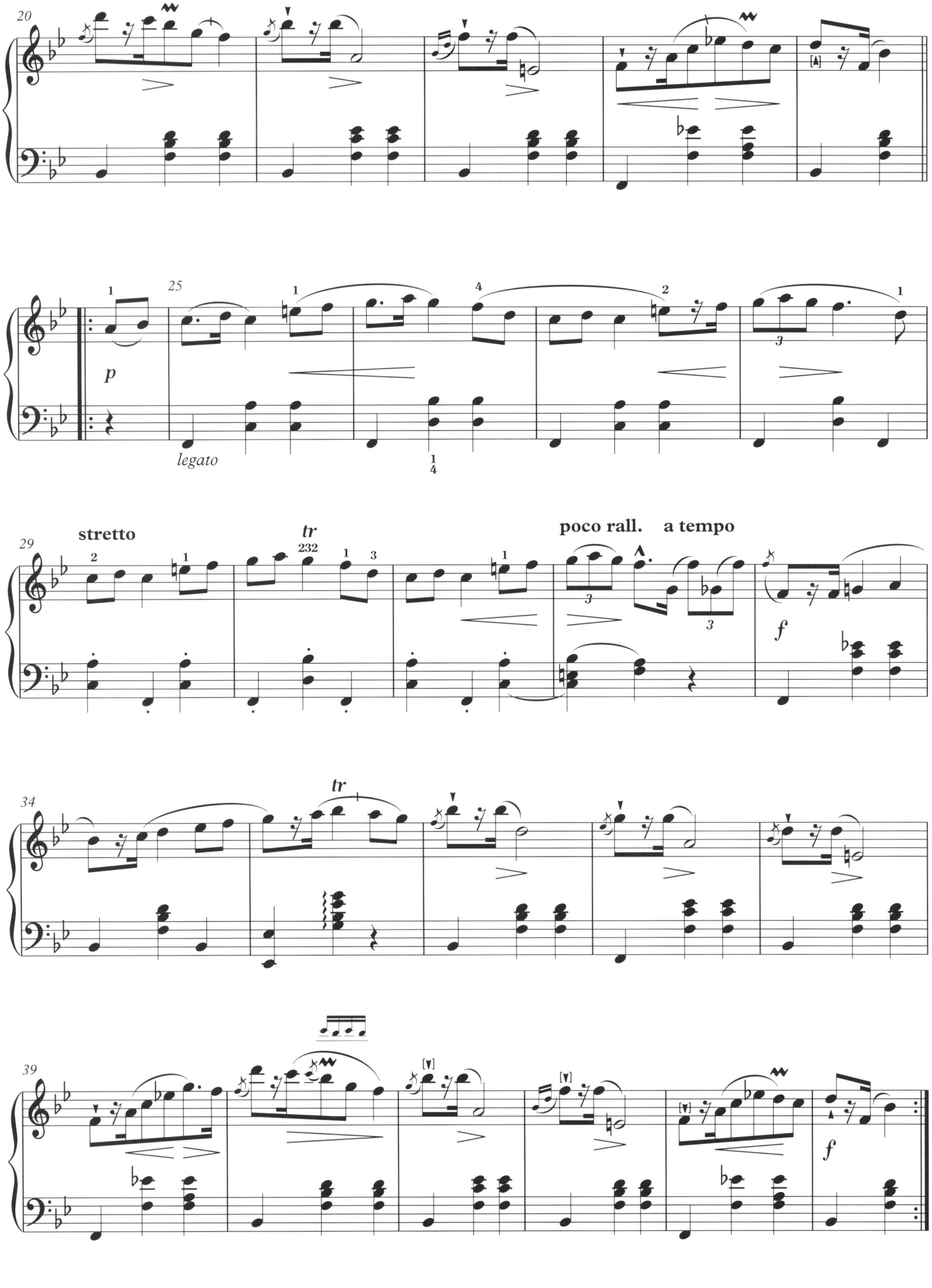
legato
stretto
poco rall.
a tempo

45
pp sotto voce
Ped.
[sim.]
49
rubato
tr
poco rall.
a tempo
f
Ped.
54
cresc.
tr
ff
[fz]
[p scherz.]
Ped.
58
[sim.]
62
1.
2.
f
fz
[Ped.]

Sentimental Melody

Slow Dance

Aaron Copland
(1900–1990)

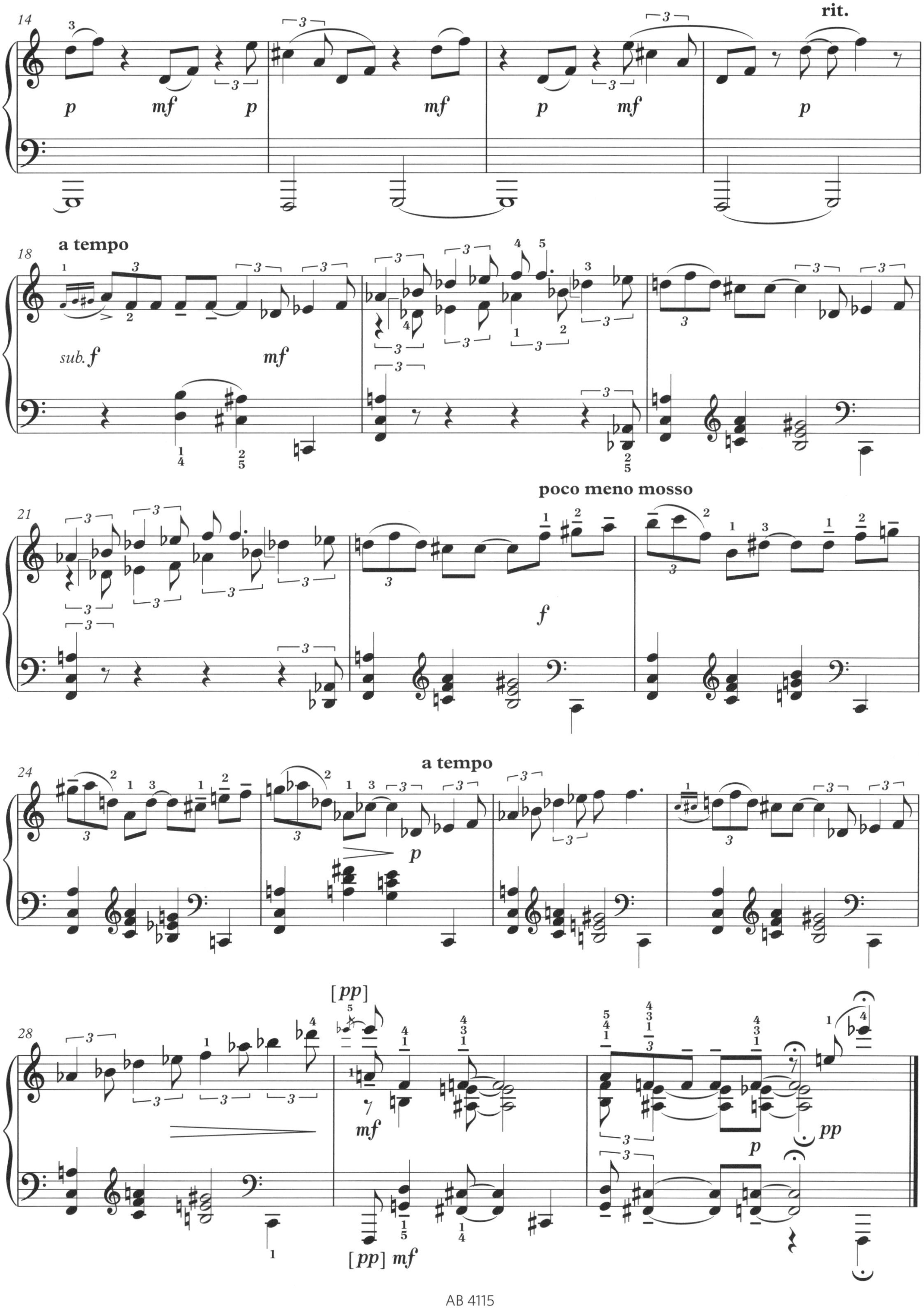
rit.
a tempo
sub. f
poco meno mosso
a tempo
[pp]
[pp] mf

The Little Shepherd

No. 5 from *Children's Corner*

Claude Debussy
(1862–1918)

Cédez
più p
au Mouvement
un poco più forte
Plus mouvementé
Poco animato
cresc.
più p
Un peu retenu
(en conservant le rythme)
Cédez

Dance on the Porch

from *Little Women*

Alexandre Desplat
(born 1961)

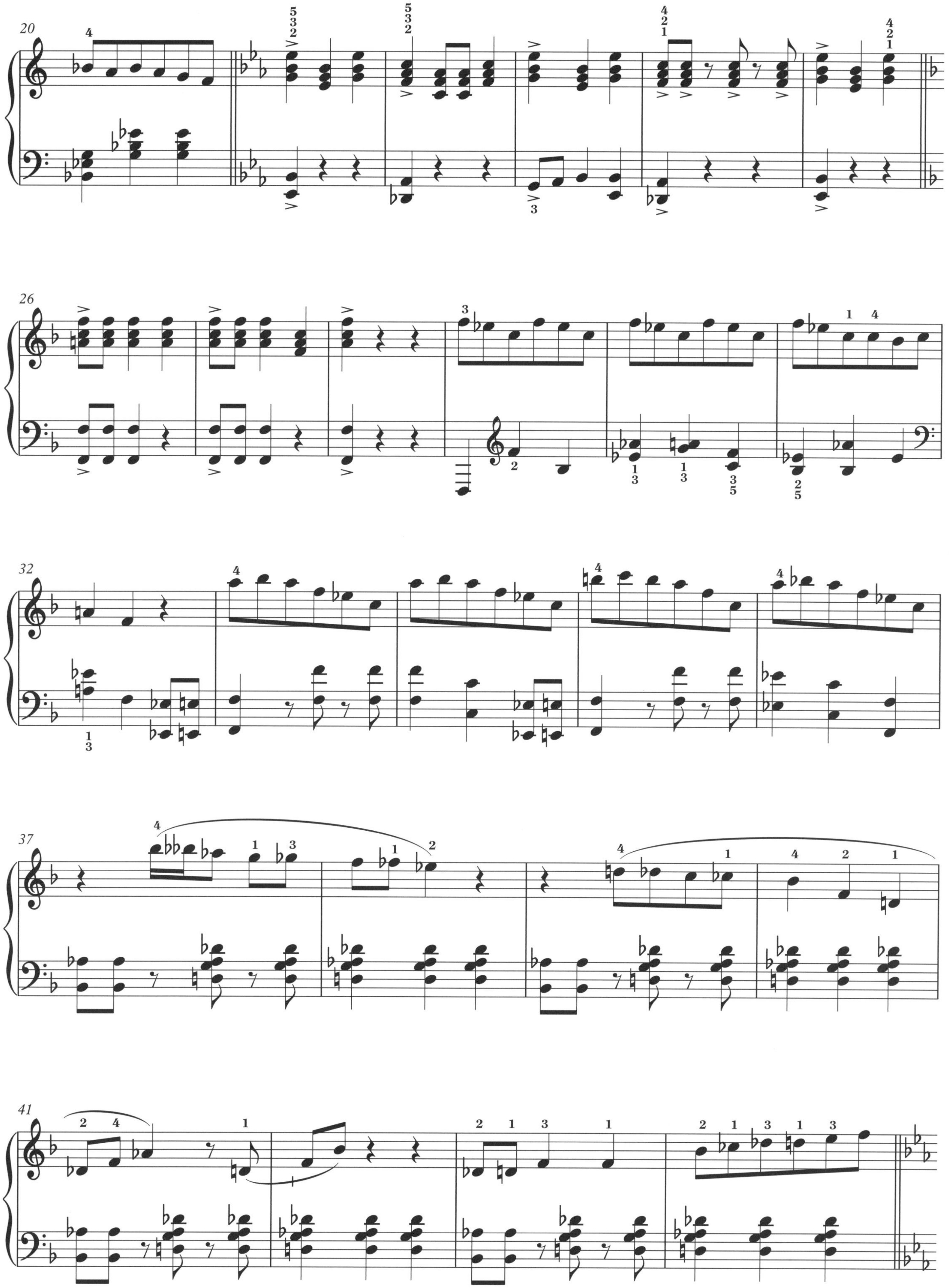

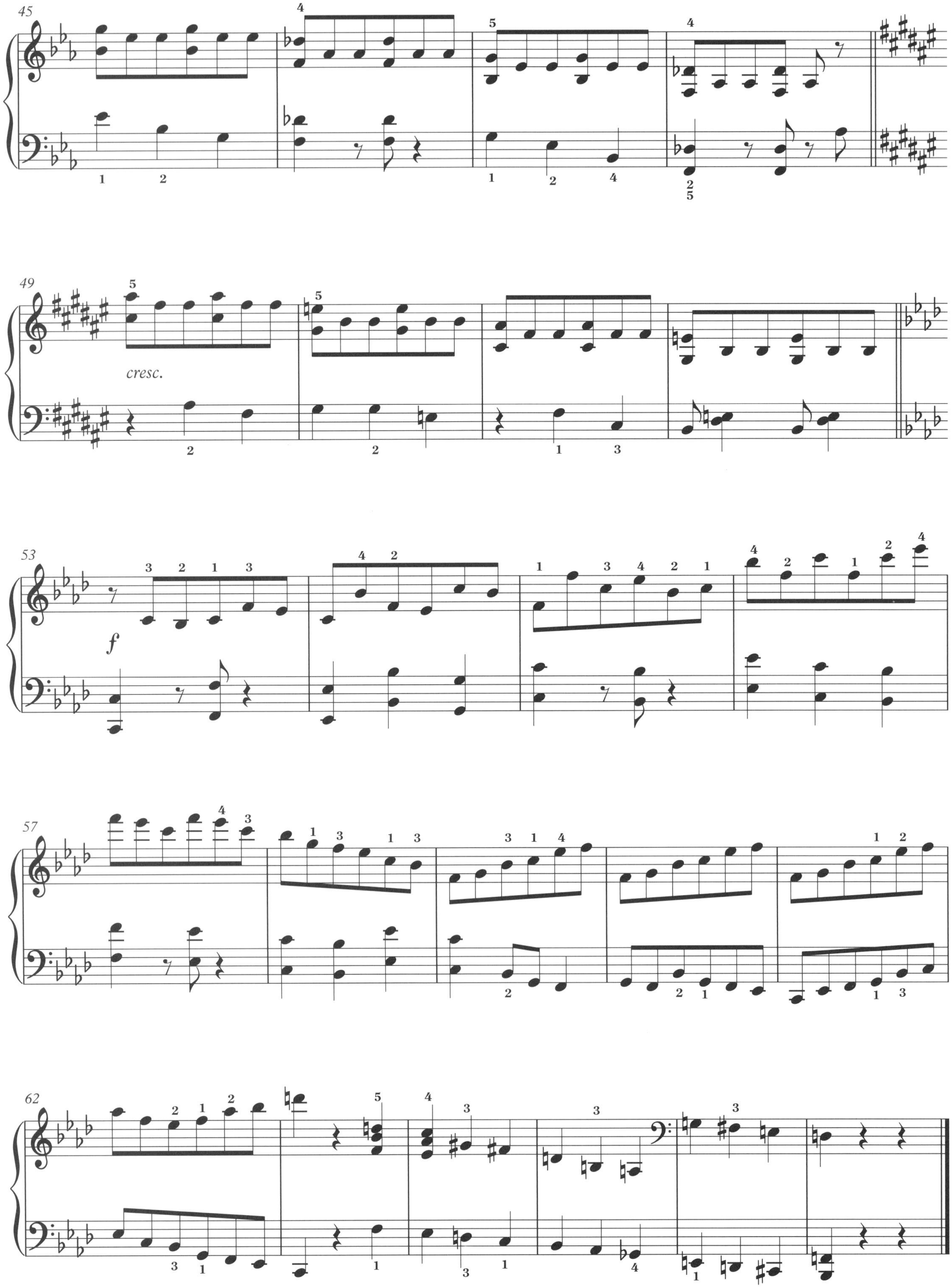
cresc.
f

Prelude

No. 7 from *Ten Pieces*, Op. 12

Sergei Prokofiev
(1891–1953)

Vivo e delicato [♩ = *c*.132]

sempre **pp**

pochissimo cresc.

p

Published by Rob. Forberg Musikverlag, part of UMPG Classics & Screen
International copyright secured. All rights reserved.
Reprinted by permission of Hal Leonard Europe BV (Italy).

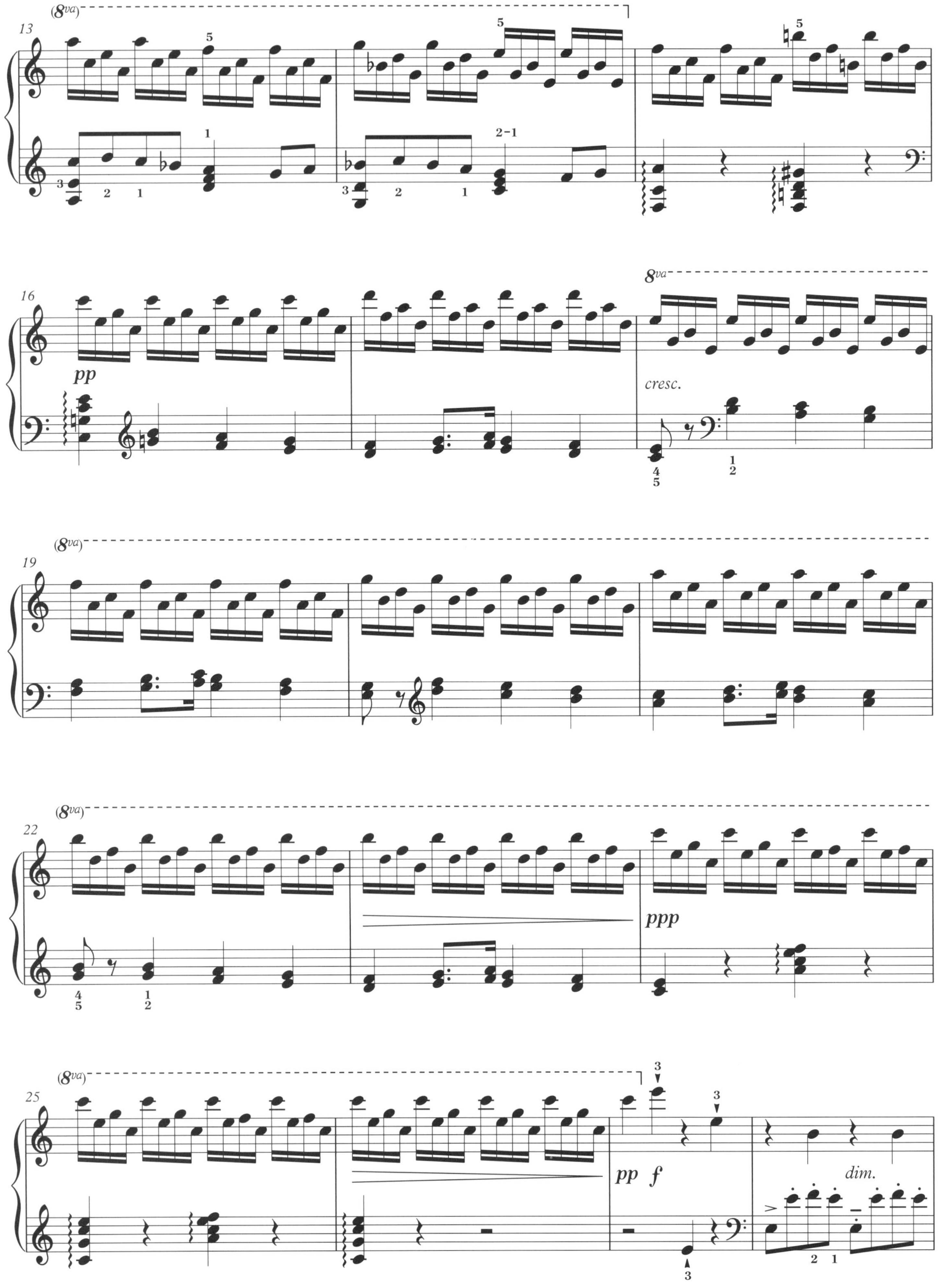
(8va)
13
16
pp
8va
cresc.
(8va)
19
(8va)
22
ppp
(8va)
25
pp
f
dim.

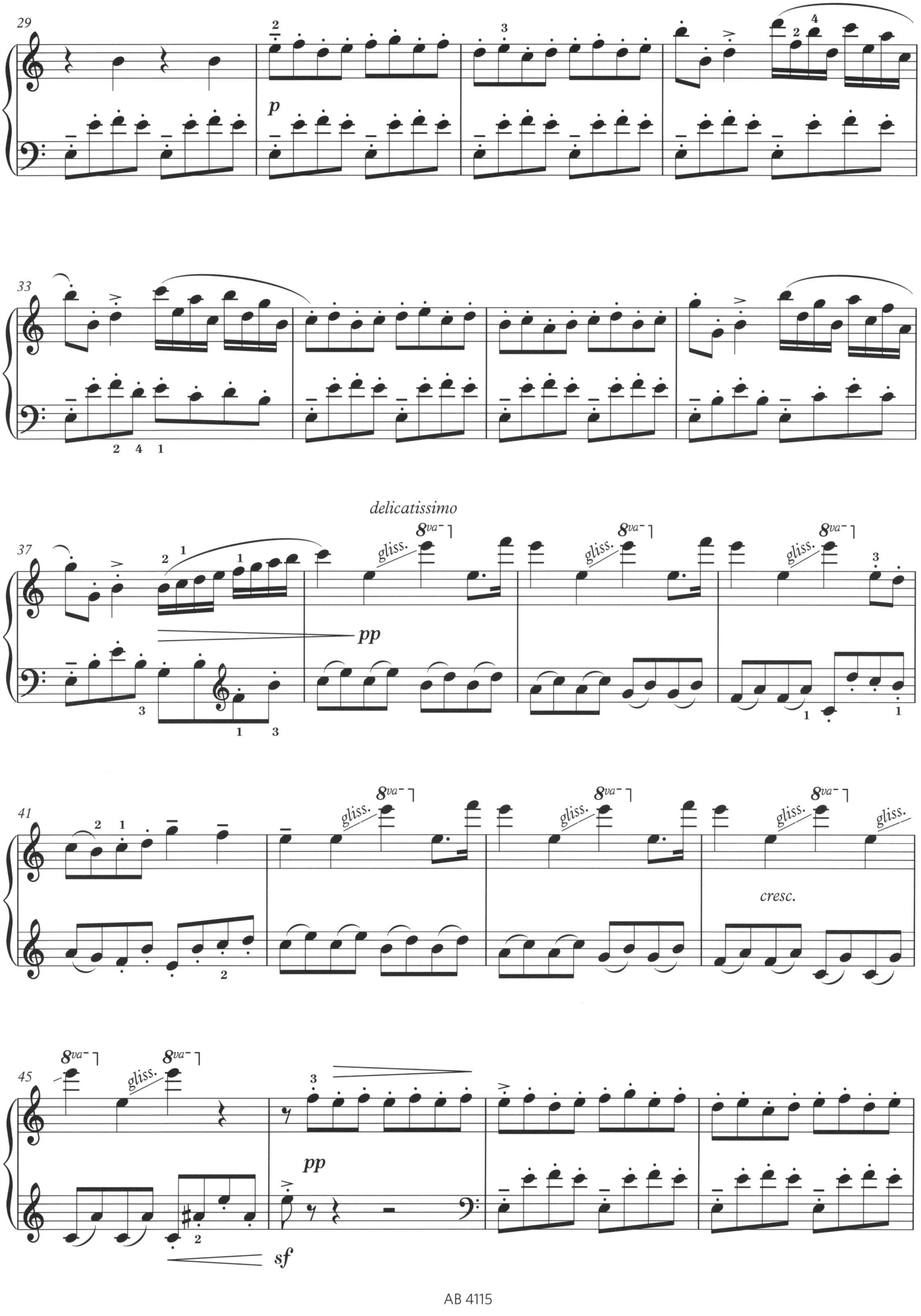
29
p
33
37
delicatissimo
gliss.
8va
pp
41
cresc.
45
sf

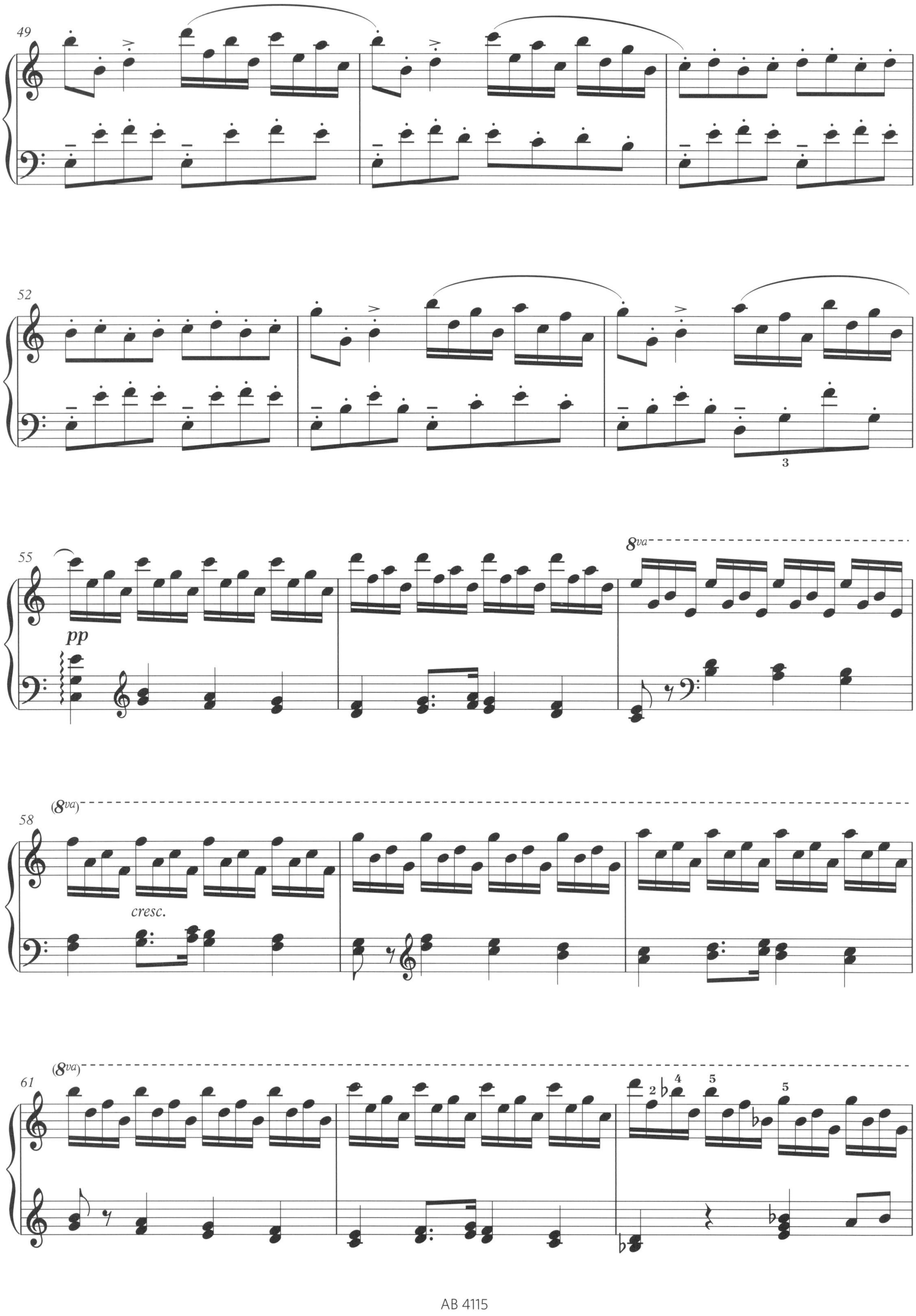
49
52
3
55
pp
8va
58
(8va)
cresc.
61
(8va)
2
4
5
5

64
(8va)
67
(8va)
70
(8va)
pp
73
76
Poco meno mosso
79
ritard.
a tempo
8va
ppp

Praeambulum

First movement from Partita No. 5, BWV 829

J. S. Bach
(1685–1750)

© 2023 by The Associated Board of the Royal Schools of Music

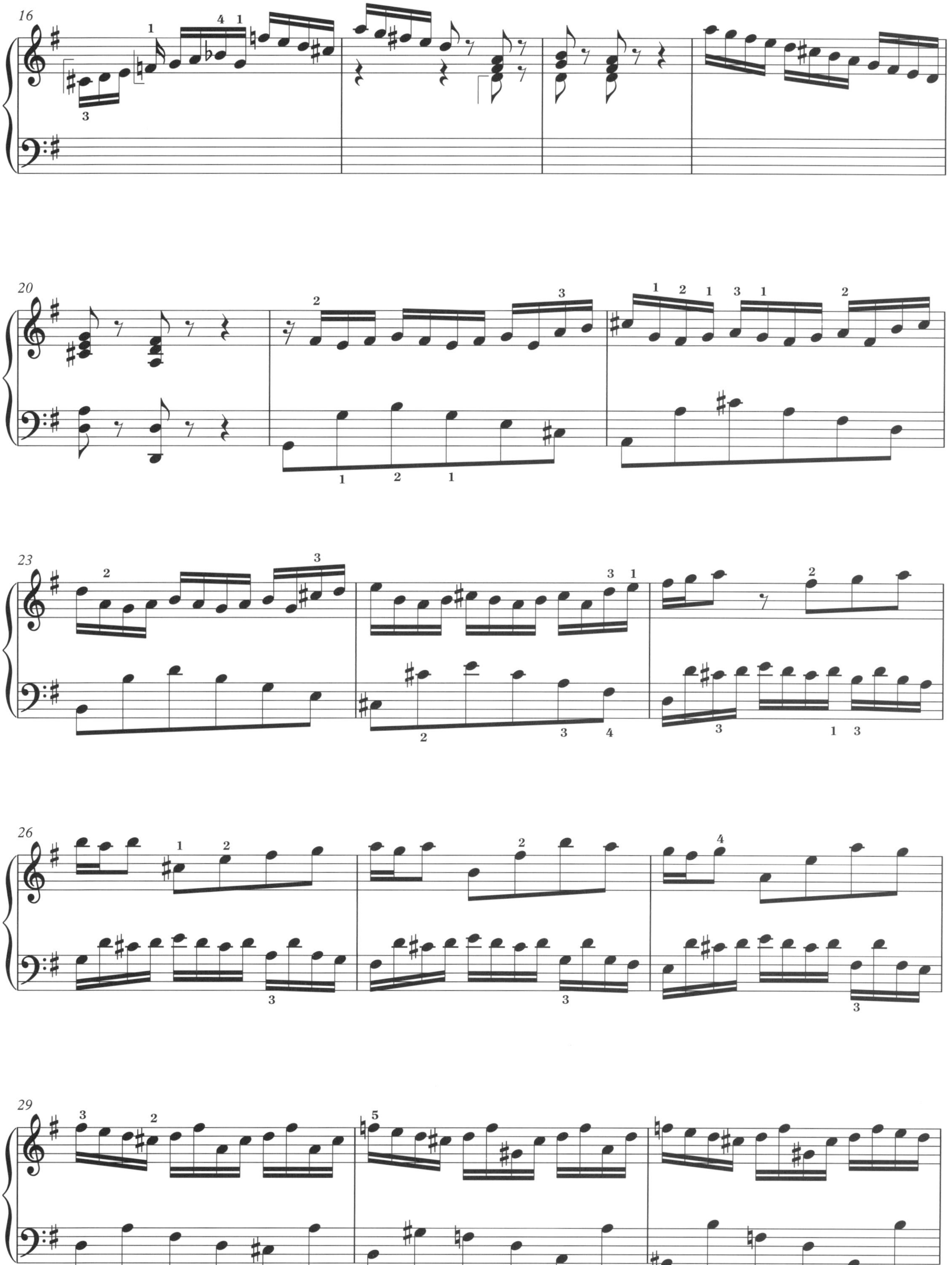
16
20
23
26
29

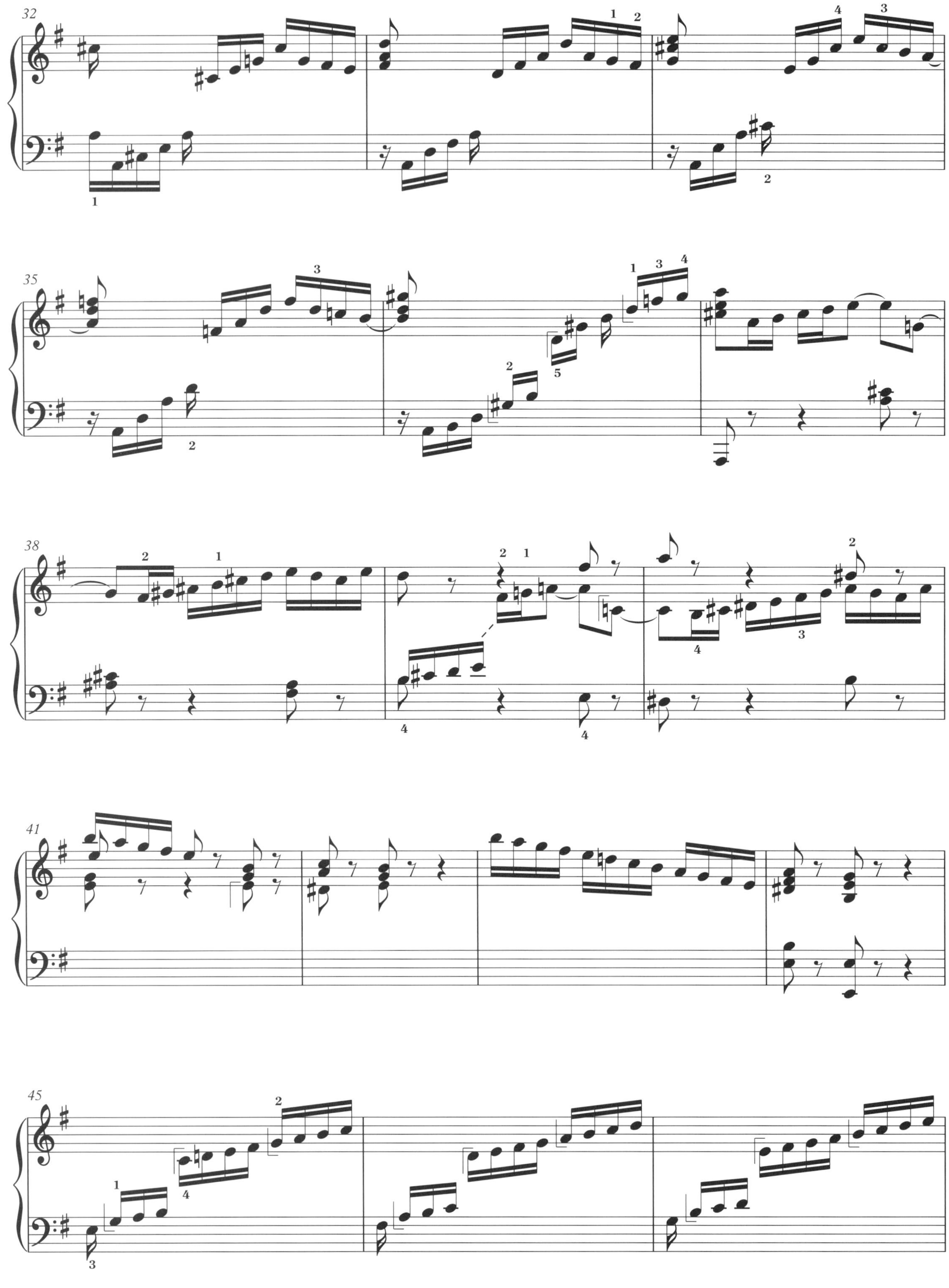

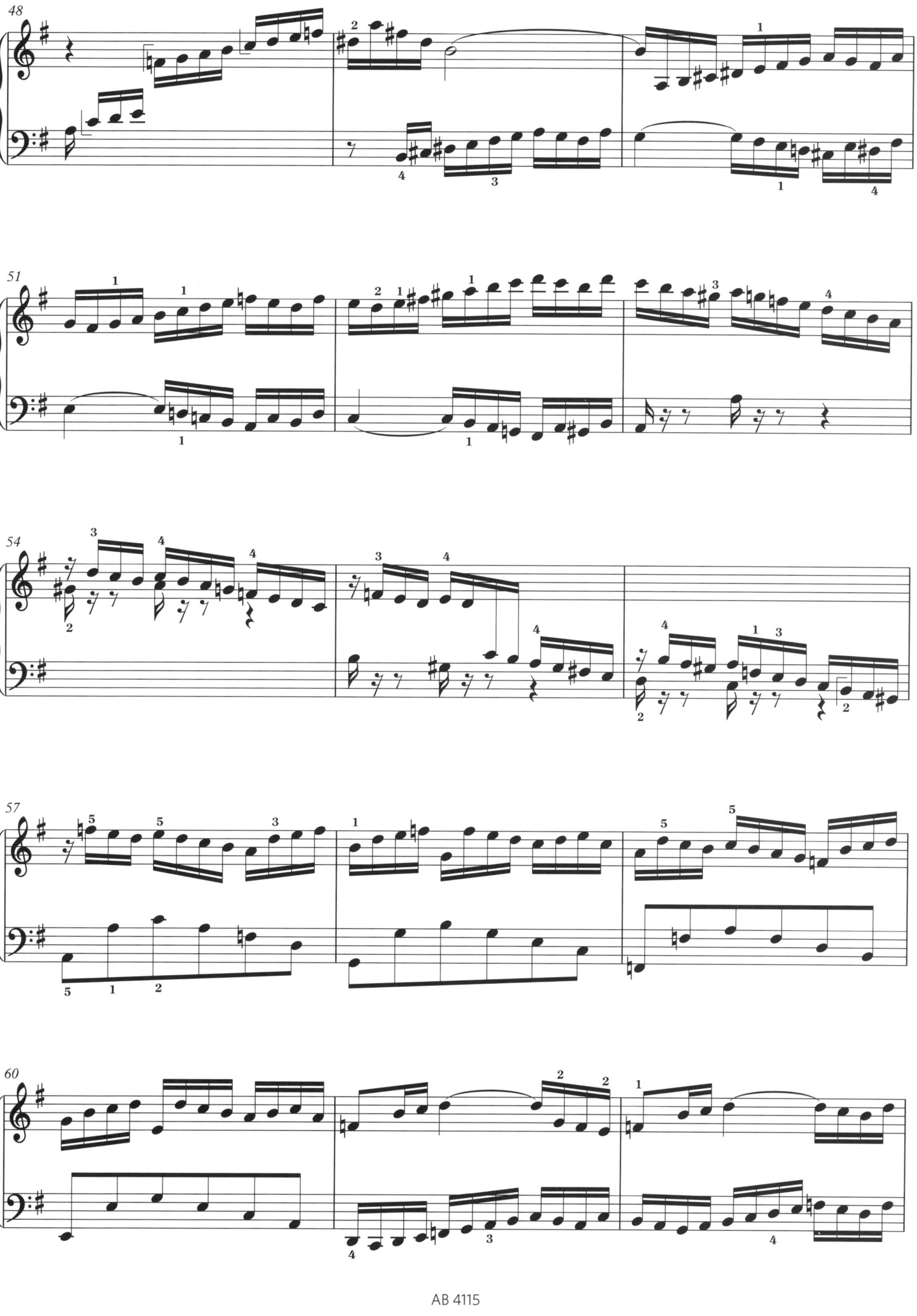
48
51
54
57
60

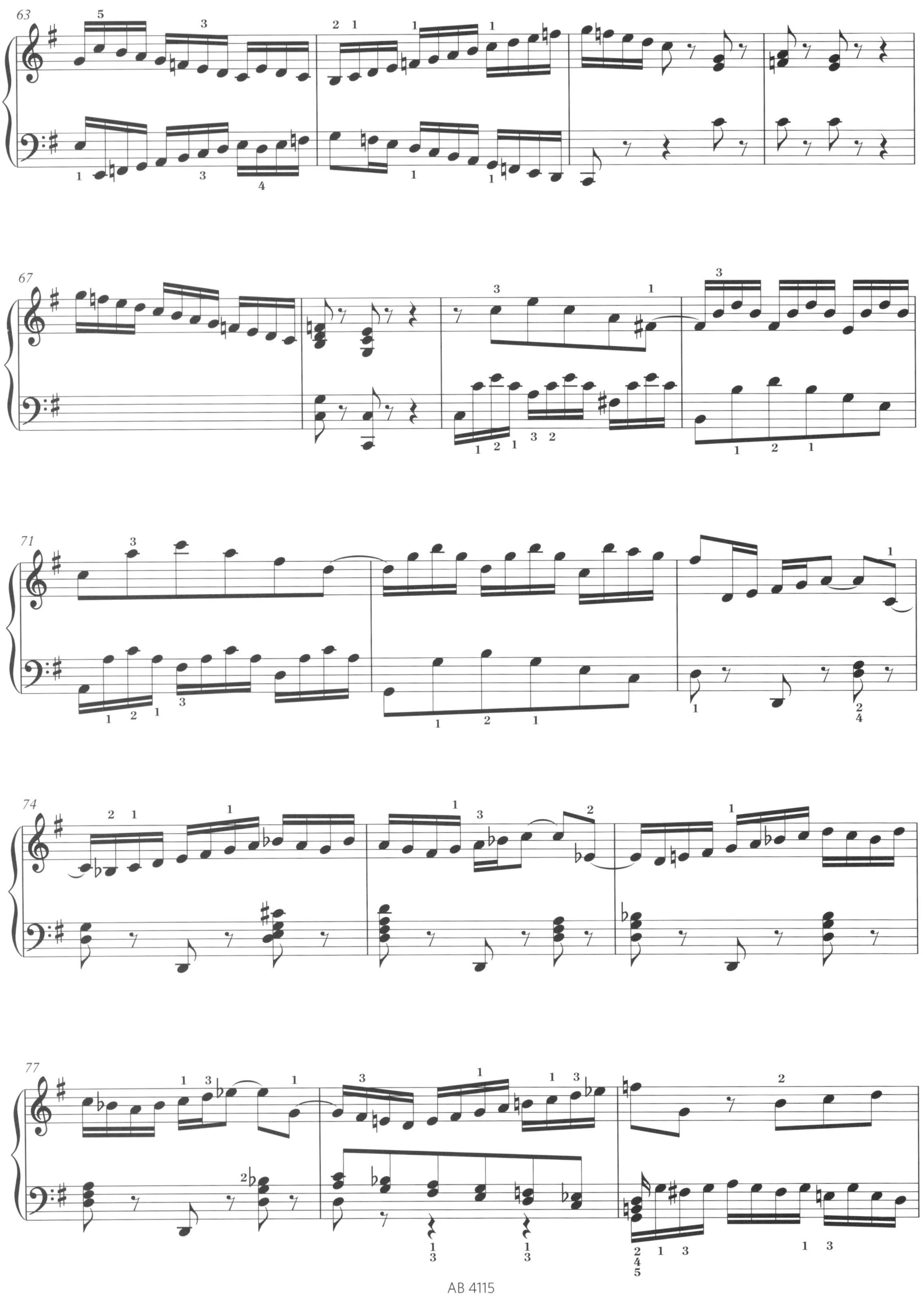
63
67
71
74
77

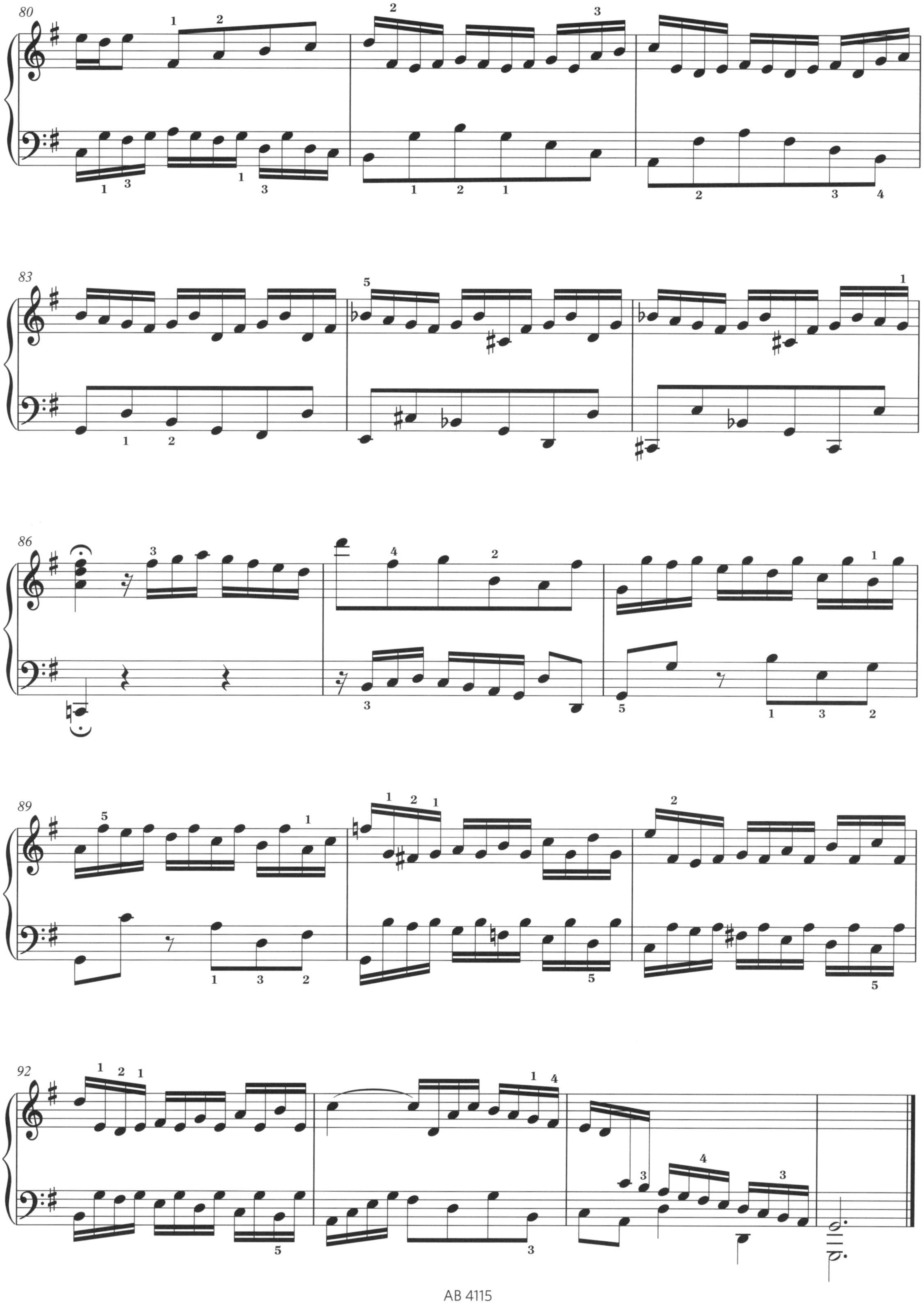

The Puppets' Dance

Tanec loutek

No. 5 from *Loutky*, Book 1

Bohuslav Martinů
(1890–1959)

© 2008 Bärenreiter Praha

AB 4115

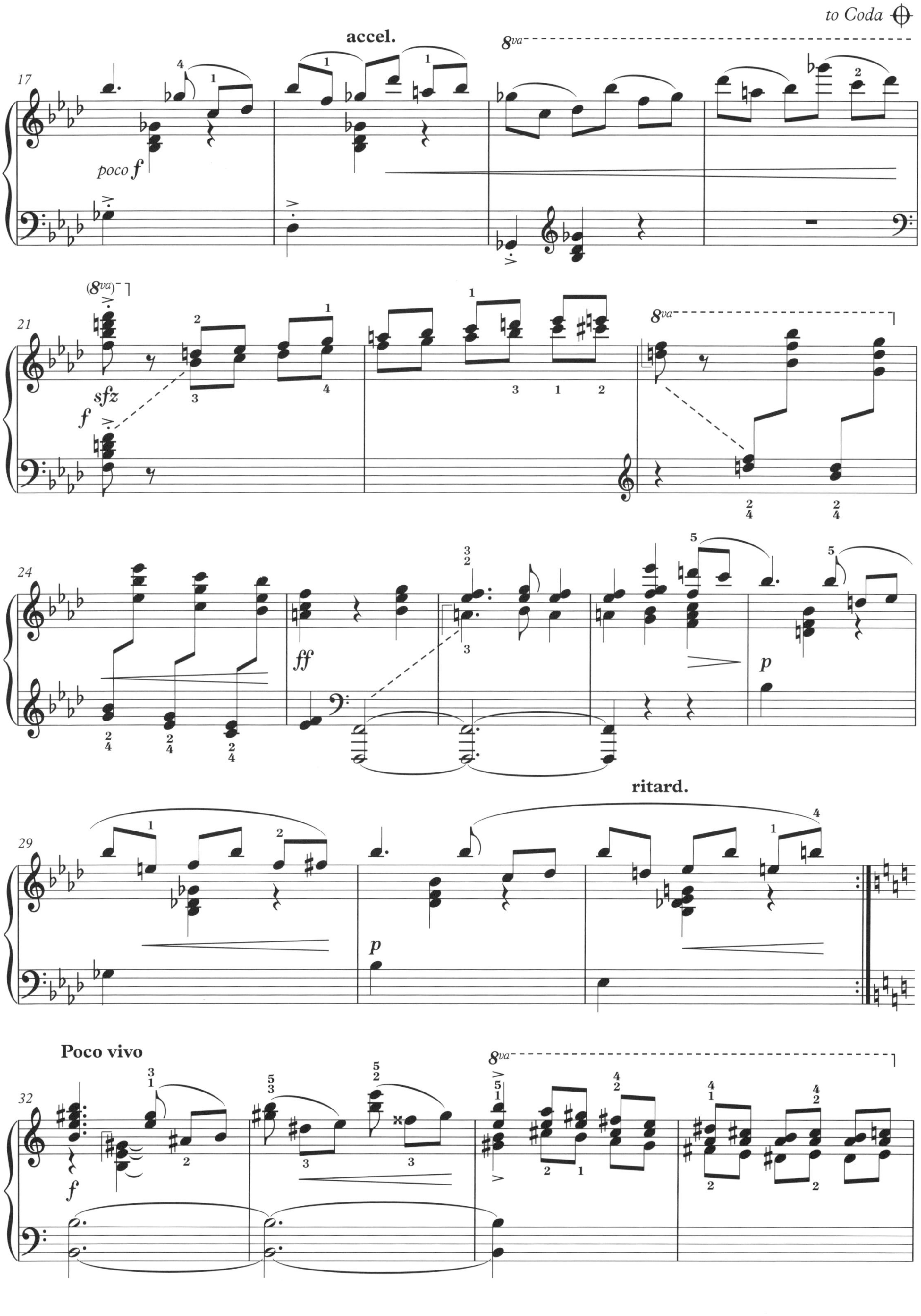
to Coda
accel.
poco f
sfz
f
ff
p
ritard.
p
Poco vivo
f

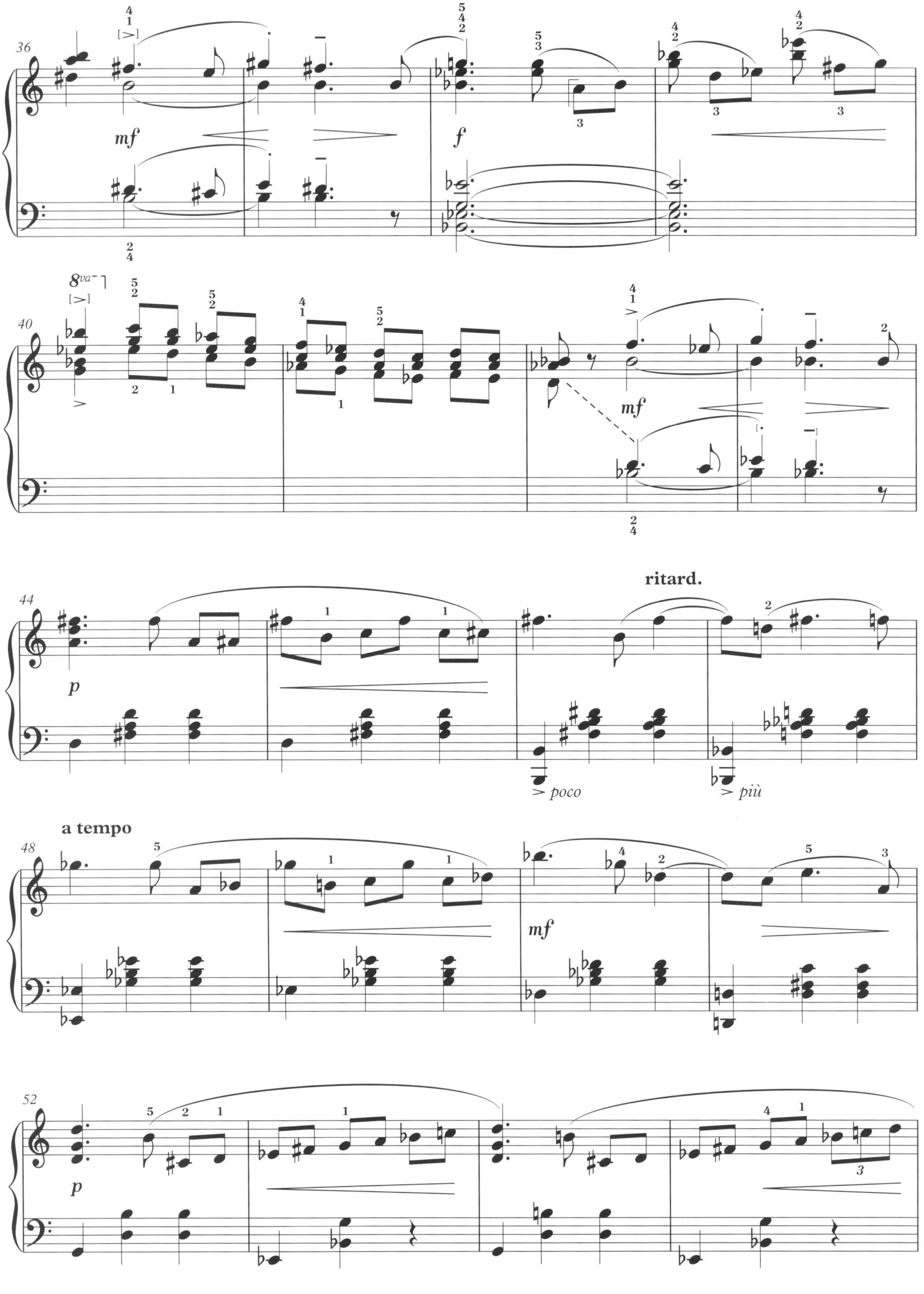
mf
f
8va
ritard.
poco
più
a tempo
p

mf
più
f
D.C. al Coda
CODA
accel. sempre
ff
sfz
ff sempre
Allegro vivo
8va

Mélodie in E major

No. 3 from *5 Morceaux de fantasie*, Op. 3

Sergei Rachmaninoff
(1873–1943)

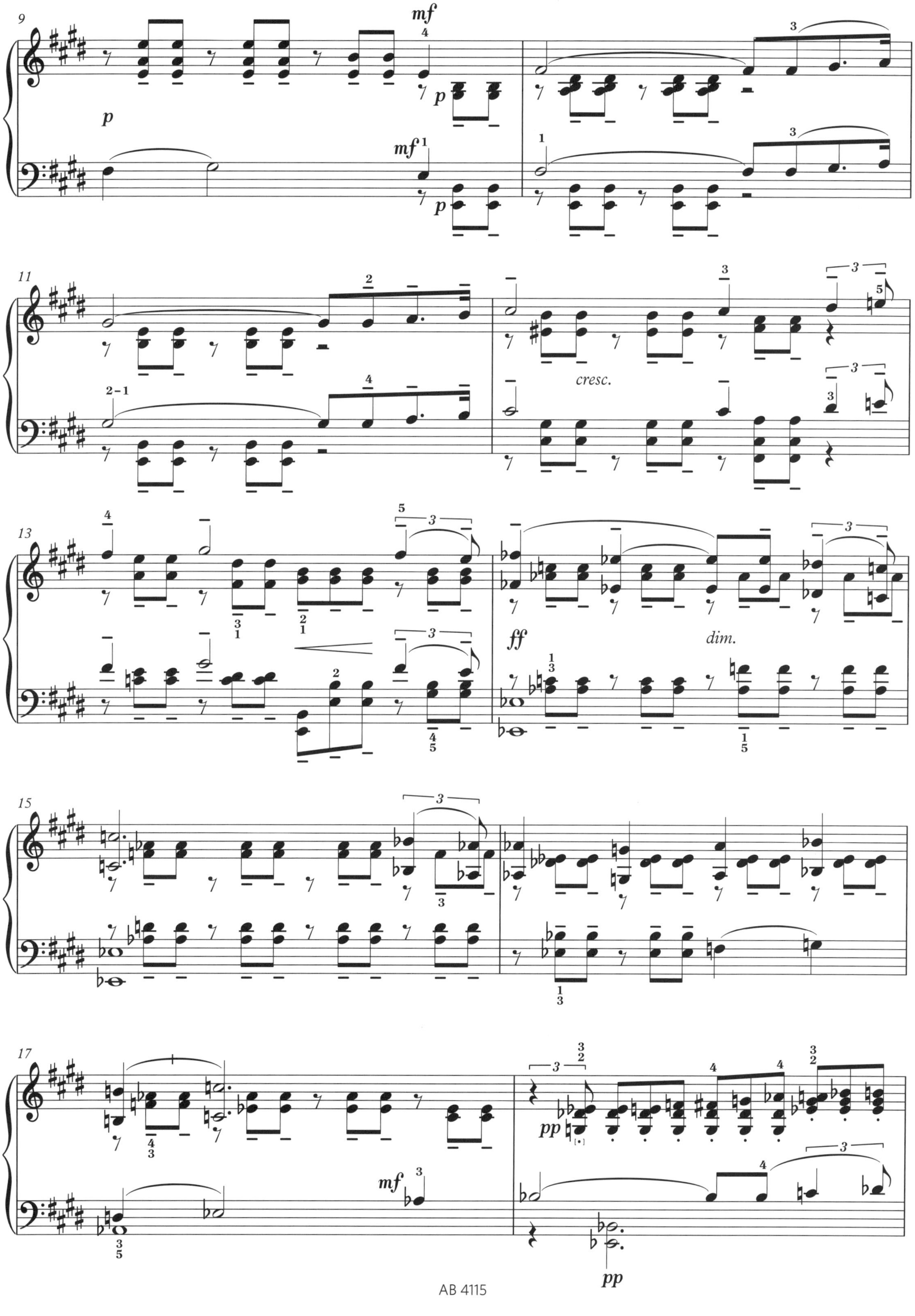
9
mf
p
mf
p
11
cresc.
13
ff
dim.
15
17
mf
pp
pp

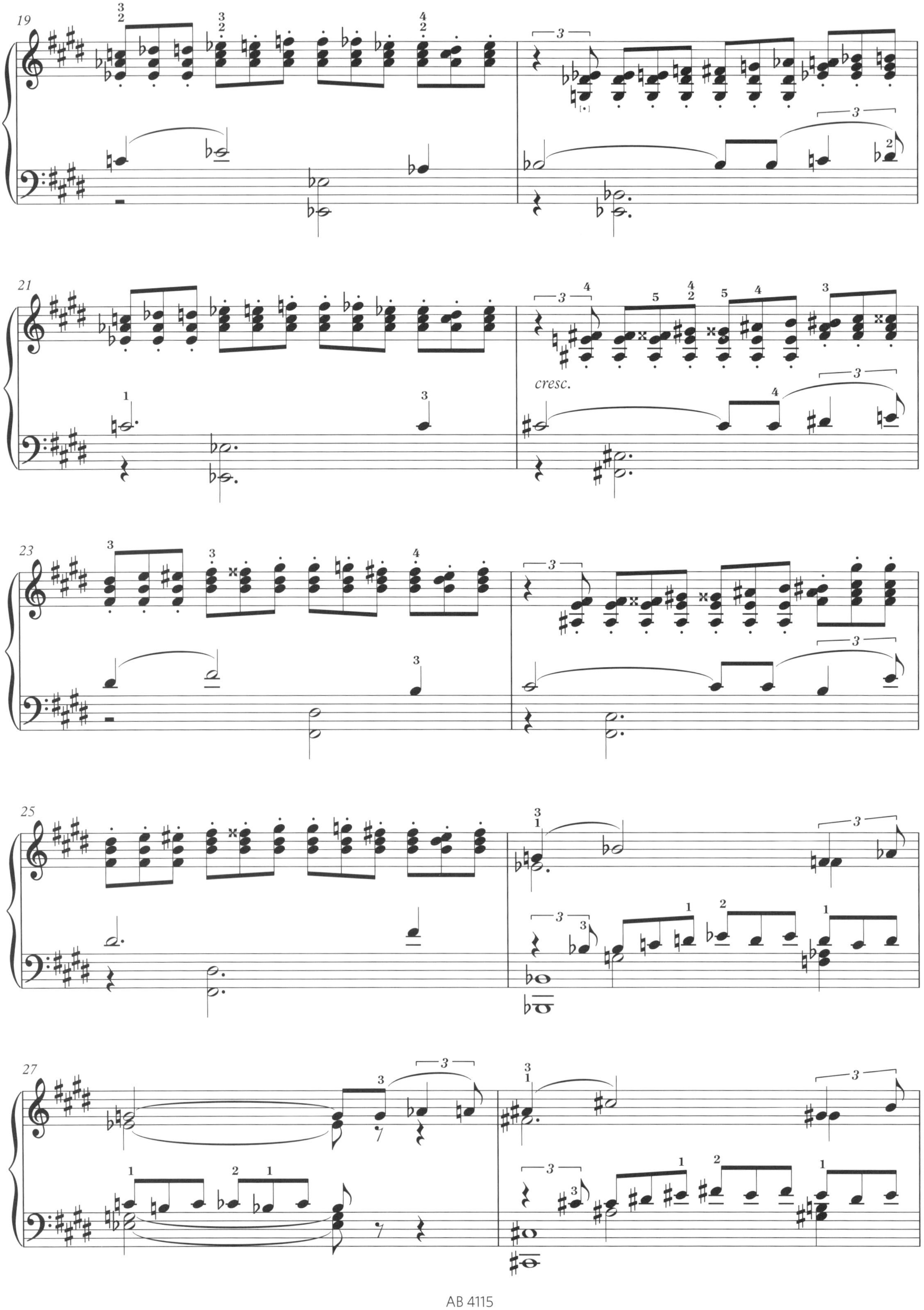
cresc.

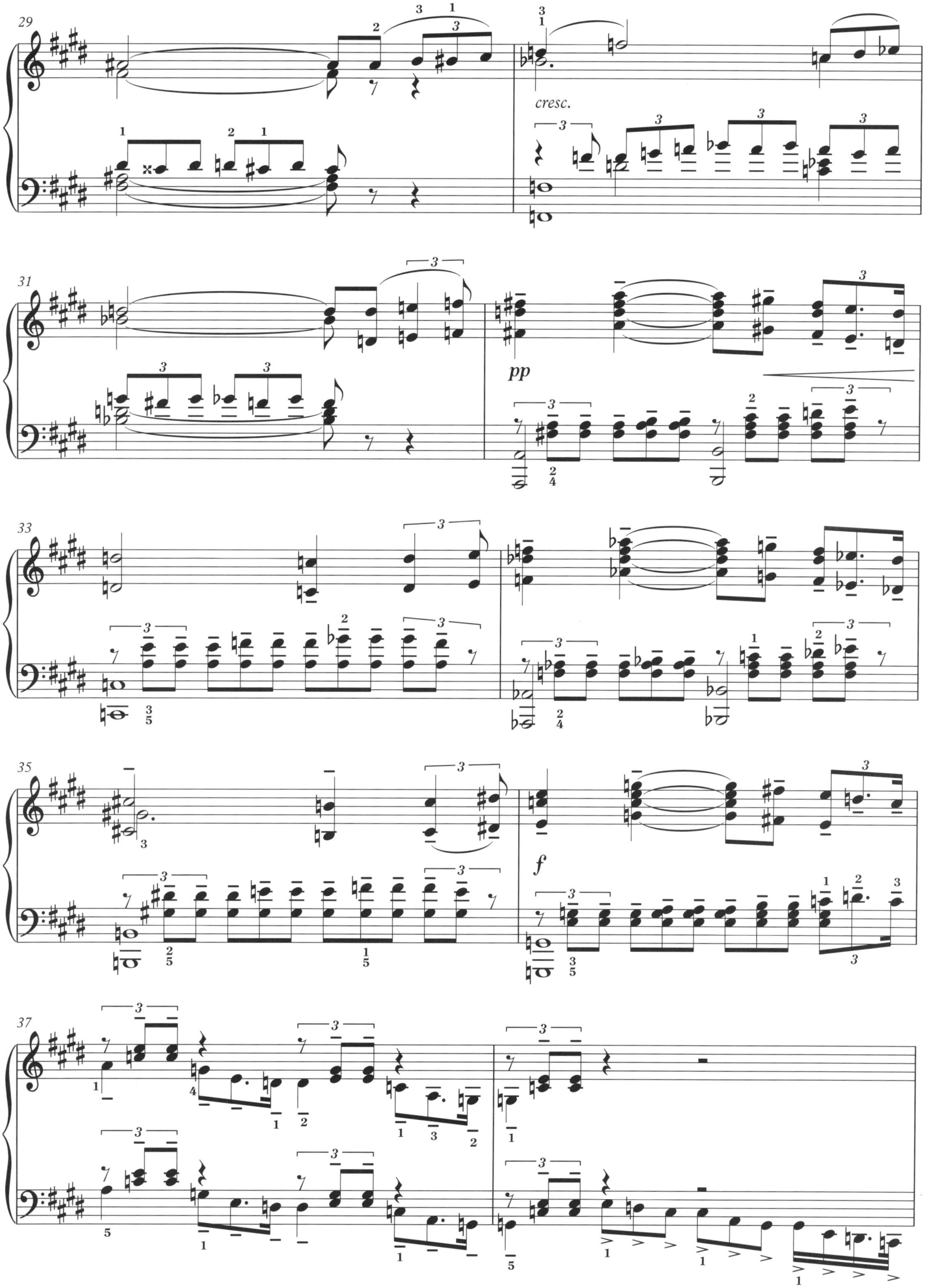
cresc.

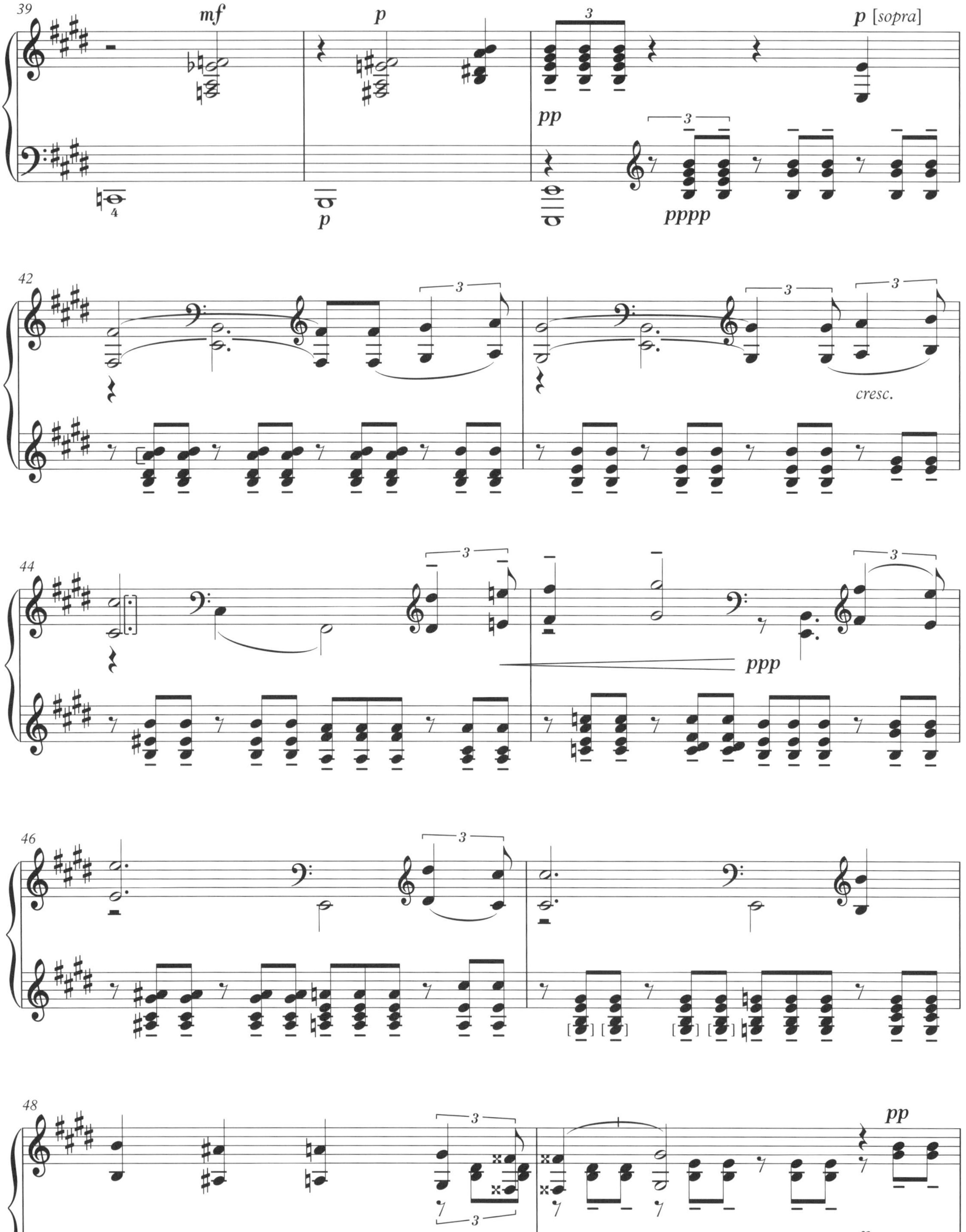
39
mf
p
3
p [sopra]
pp
3
pppp
p
42
3
3
3
cresc.
44
3
3
ppp
46
3
48
3
pp
3
p

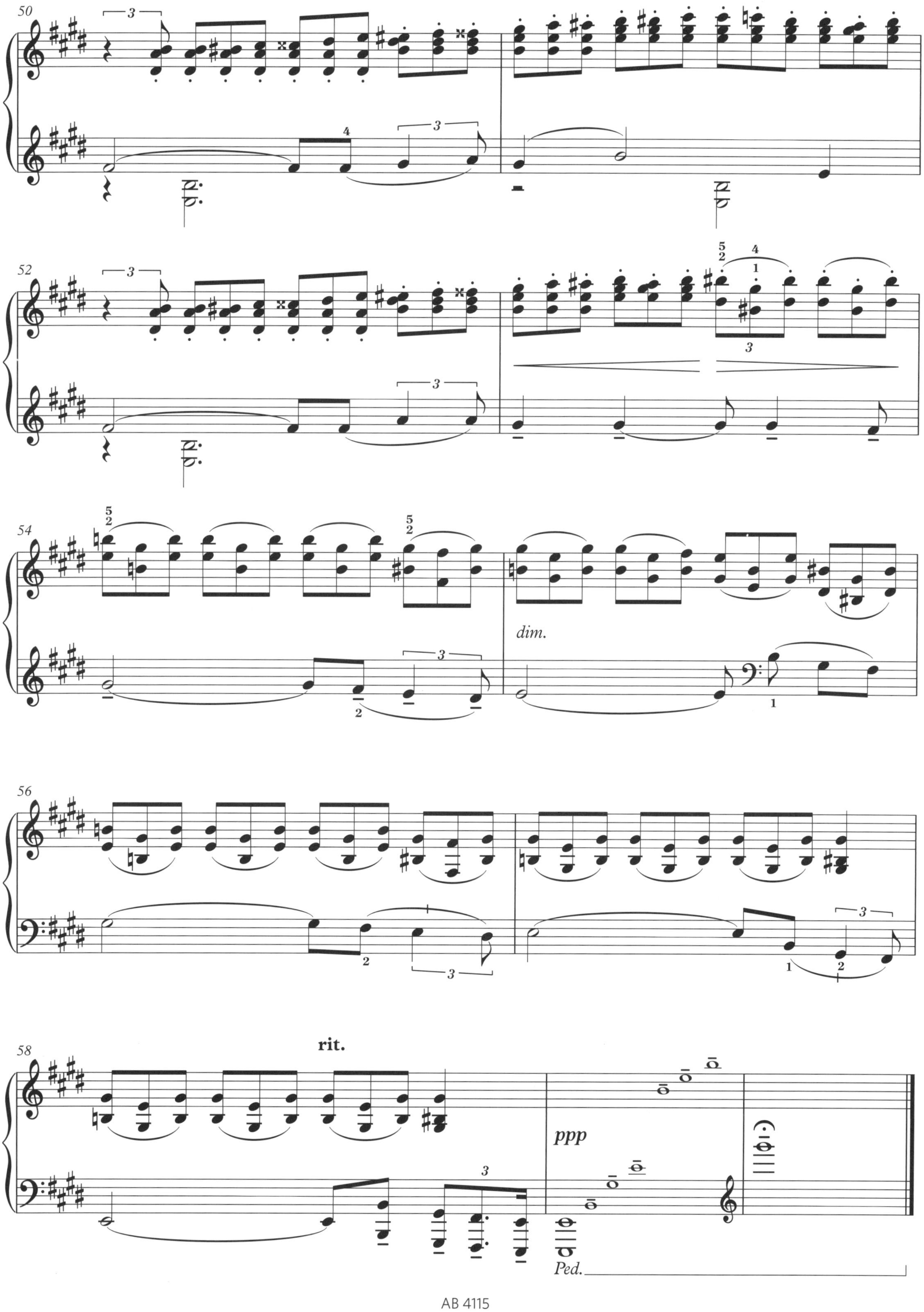
dim.
rit.
ppp
Ped.

Notturno

No. 2 from *Soirées musicales*, Op. 6

Clara Schumann
(1819–96)

* *pf* = poco forte [slightly loud]

© 2023 by The Associated Board of the Royal Schools of Music

[sim.]
cresc.
f risoluto
rinforz.
Ped.
stretto e rubato
riten.
cresc.

con grazia
p
pp
ff risolute con forza
sf
più mosso
cresc.
[sim.]
dim.

animato rinf. rit.
mf
f
Ped.
p espress.
Tempo primo
dolente
pp
calando
ppp
pf
8va
loco
cresc.
ff risoluto
p
dolce
ben marcato il canto

stretto
cresc.
riten.
ritard.
a tempo ma più lento
con espress.
calando e morendo
Ped.

Deep River

No. 10 from *24 African American Melodies*, Op. 59

Samuel Coleridge-Taylor
(1875–1912)

poco rit.
a tempo
pp
f
dim.
rall.
pp
Più mosso
mf
cresc. molto
poco tranquillo
pesante sf
sf
mp

Meno mosso (più tranquillo)

accel.

Più mosso

poco tranquillo

rall.
Più mosso
f
largamente
sf
rall.
sf
Tempo primo
pp
pp
poco rit.
[a tempo]
mf

poco rit.
a tempo
55
f
dim.
58
f
dim.
poco rit.
pp
più tranquillo
61
pp
dim.
63
morendo
mf
65
pp
8va

Prelude No. 1

from *Three Preludes*

George Gershwin
(1898–1937)

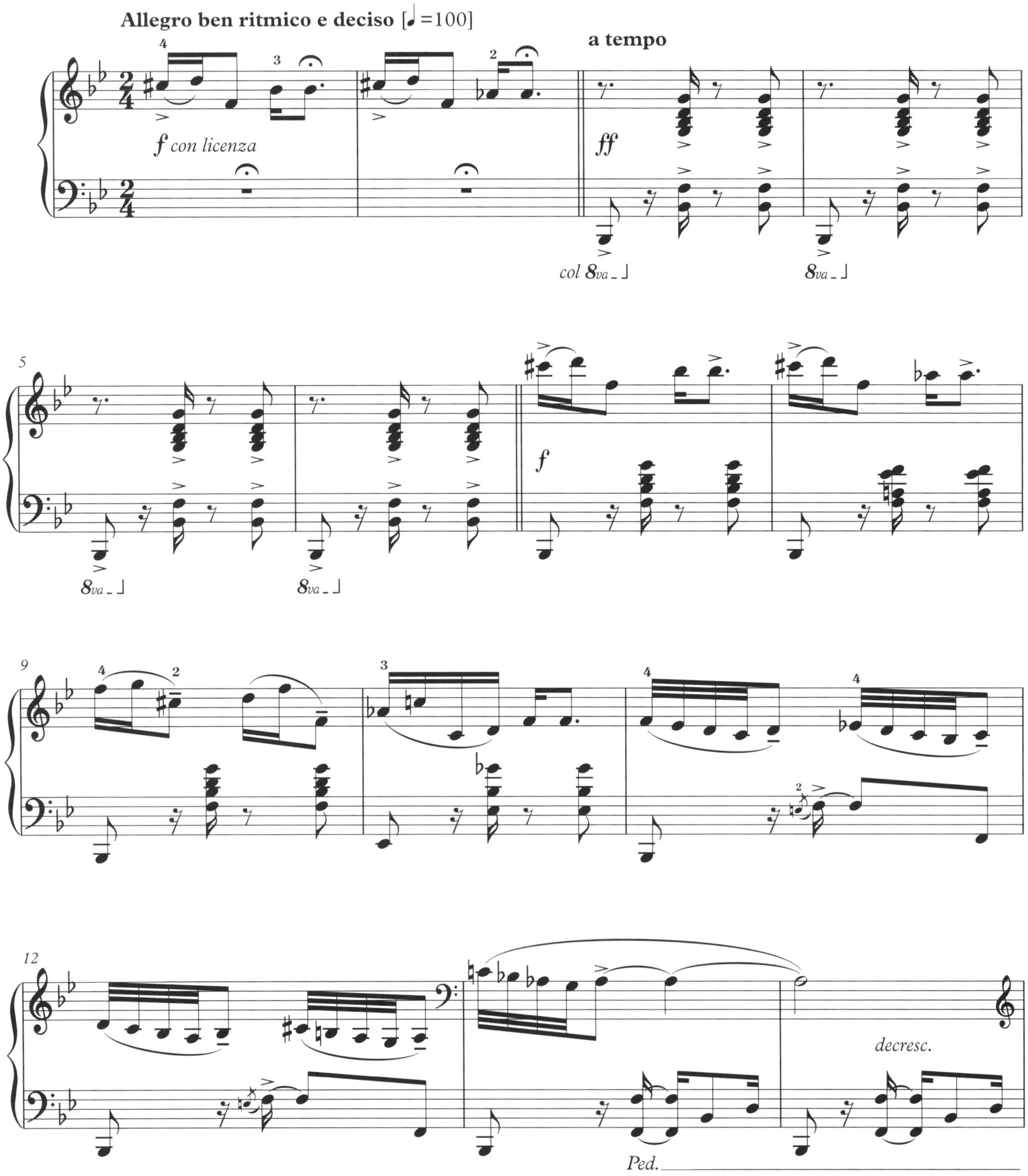

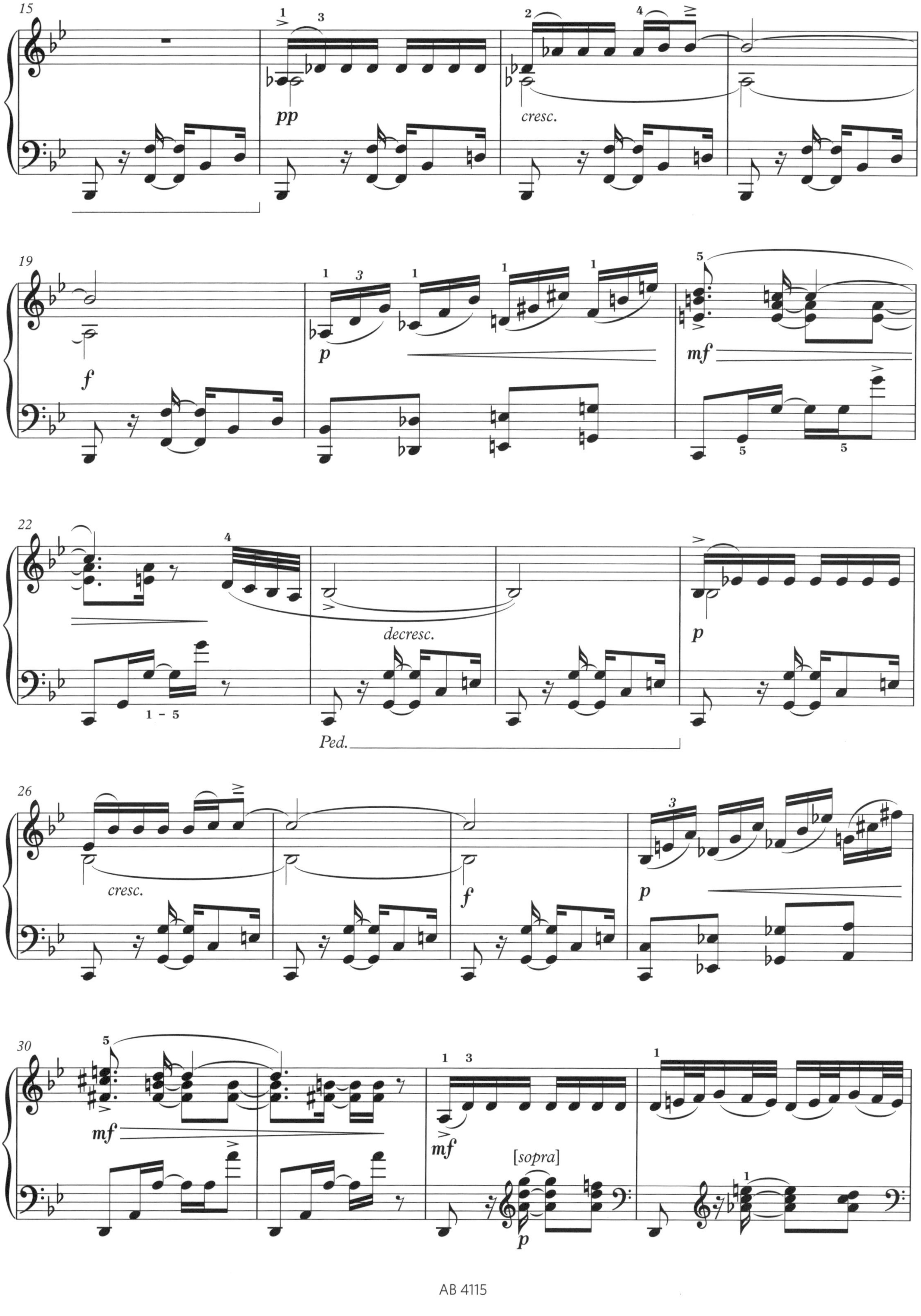
15
pp
cresc.
19
f
p
mf
22
decresc.
Ped.
p
26
cresc.
f
p
30
mf
mf
[sopra]
p

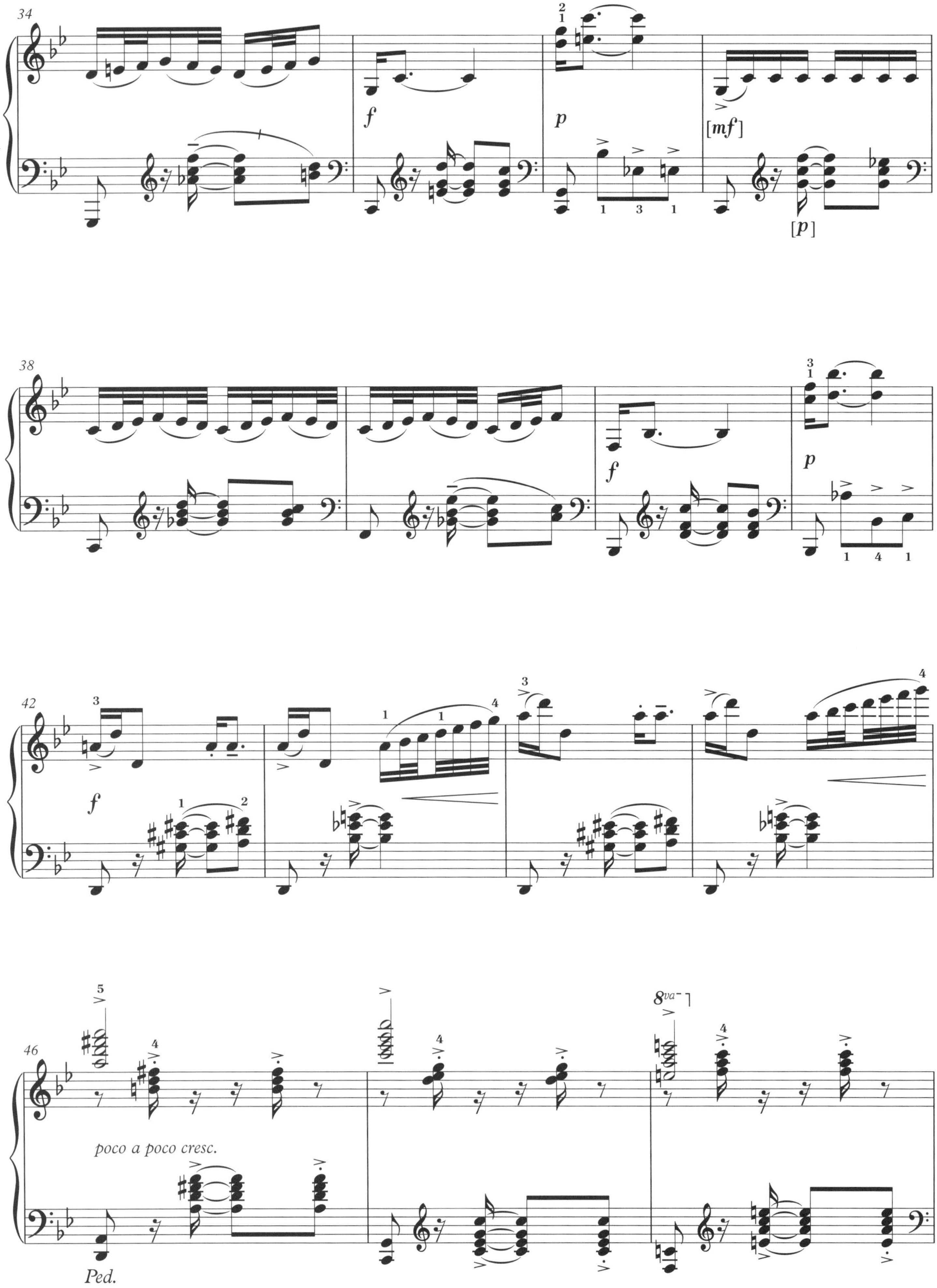
poco a poco cresc.
Ped.
8va

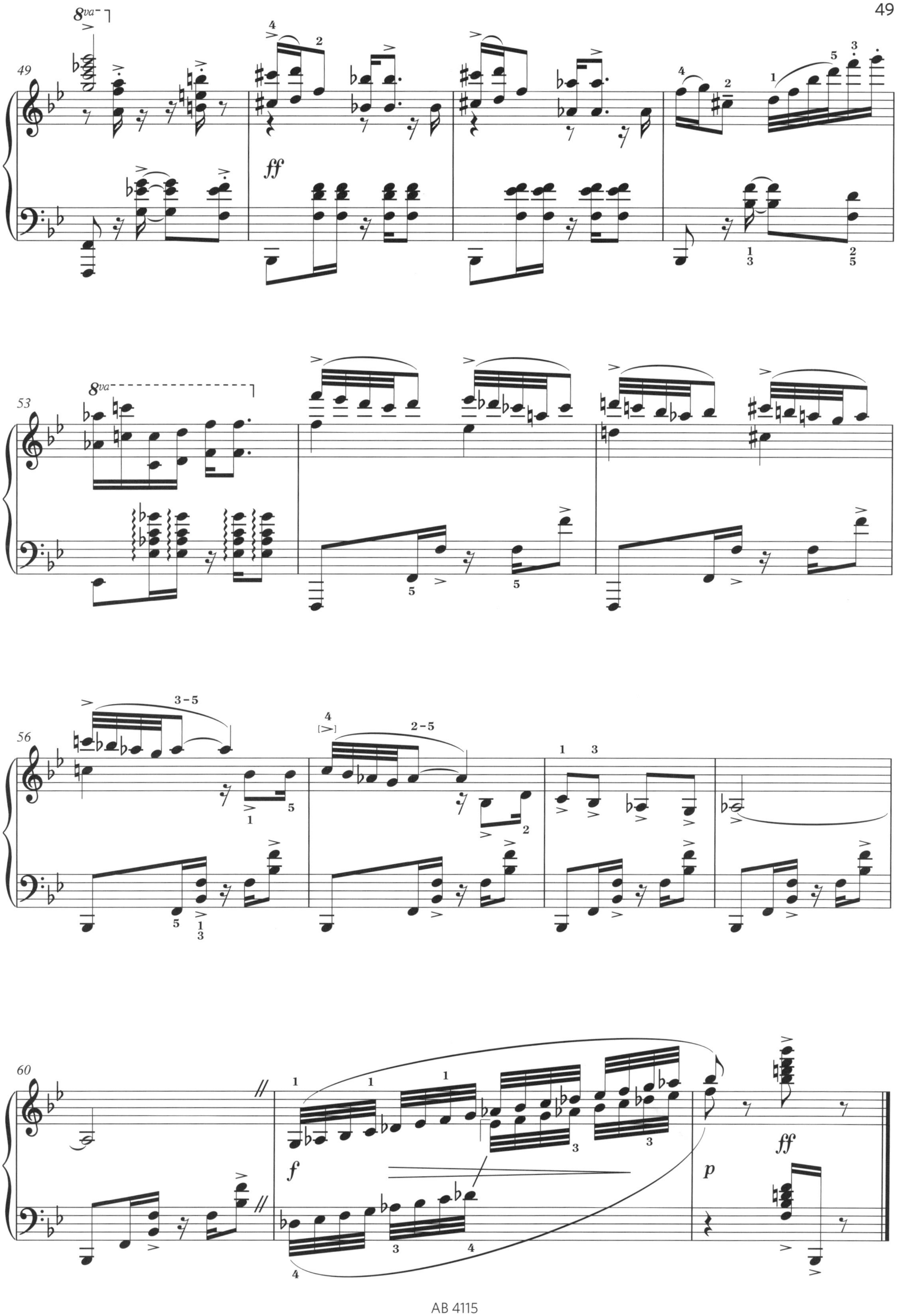
49
8va
ff
53
8va
56
60
f
p
ff

for Isata

Dream

Errollyn Wallen
(born 1958)

p
f
Ped.
rall.
a tempo
slow arpegg.
mf
mp cantabile e espressivo
pp

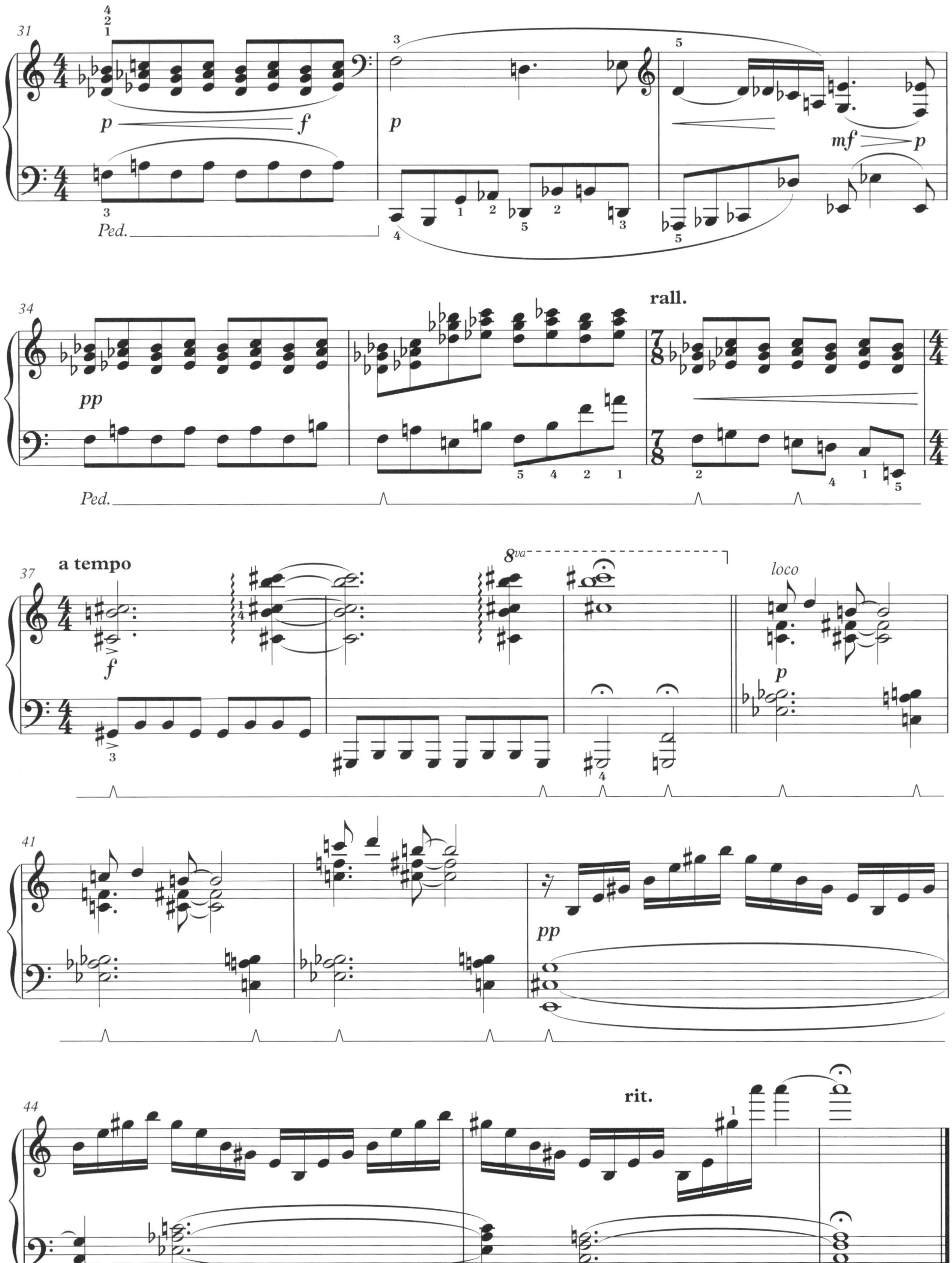

p
f
Ped.
p
mf
p
pp
Ped.
rall.
a tempo
f
8va
loco
p
pp
rit.